ROSA PARKS

From the Back of the Bus to the Front of a Movement

by Camilla Wilson

SCHOLASTIC INC.

New York   Toronto   London   Auckland   Sydney
Mexico City   New Delhi   Hong Kong

PHOTO CREDITS

Front cover: UPI / Corbis.
Interior insert:
#1-#5: AP / Wide World #6 UPI / Corbis #7,
#8 AP / Wide World

ISBN 0-439-16330-7

12 11 10 9 8 7 6 5 4   1 2 3 4 5 6/0
                                                    40
Printed in the U.S.A.

First Scholastic printing, January 2001

Acknowledgments

I have been blessed with the support and assistance of numerous people on this project. In particular, I would like to thank Dr. Linda Ferreira, editorial director at Scholastic, for first mentioning the project to me; Kate Egan, my editor, for her patience and assistance; and Rod Miller and Kristen James for their excellent research.

The staff at Tuskegee University and the George Washington Carver Museum provided me with much information and directed me to additional sources.

Eric Johnson's computer expertise was invaluable. Tristine Rainer's writing hints kept me focused. Terry Condon and George Holland provided much assistance during revisions.

Dr. Marian Huttenstine encouraged my project and gave me a sense of the legal climate in Alabama during the civil rights struggle. Donna Blair dispensed critical assistance on numerous occasions.

Joe Holloway, an extraordinary Alabama photographer, gave me a superb tour of Montgomery, allowing me to visualize events as they took place a half-century ago. Anne Holloway provided both hospitality and succor to the project.

Judith Adams, Kate Permenter, Merry George, and Pamela Thames have served as a much-appreciated cheering squad. And my daughter, Leigh Wilson-Mattson, has been both understanding of my time demands and my great champion.

I thank you all.

Camilla J. Wilson
Starkville, MS
August 5, 2000

Dedicated to my daughter,
Leigh K. Wilson-Mattson

Table of Contents

Introduction

C an you answer this riddle: When did *not* making a move result in a great American movement?

Answer: When Rosa Parks refused to move to the back of an Alabama bus. This single non-action on December 1, 1955, sparked the American Civil Rights movement and made Parks world-famous.

This book tells the story that most people don't know about Rosa Parks. This act of rebellion on the bus did not happen because Parks was tired that day or because her feet hurt. It didn't happen because she was carrying some heavy bags. Instead, it was one more quiet, simple act of protest — the kind she had been making all her life.

Rosa Parks spent her early life in the tiny rural village of Pine Level, Alabama. As a child there, Parks faced all the aspects of segregation — the system of keeping blacks and whites as separate as possible. This system also kept blacks in the worst jobs and put them at constant risk of violence.

Even as a young child Rosa Parks wanted to be treated just like any other little girl. But this was a lot to ask in a community where black children were not treated the same as white children, and black adults were not treated the same as white adults.

On a chilly day in Montgomery, Alabama, Rosa Parks refused a white bus driver's order to give up her seat to a white passenger and move to the back of the bus. Her action ignited a bus boycott in Montgomery, a year-long refusal of blacks to ride the city buses. This is considered the beginning of the civil rights movement and the end of segregation on public buses throughout the United States. The civil rights movement challenged the existing system of segregation in housing, restaurants, schools, and jobs. It led to the passage of many issues banning unequal treatment of the races and, eventually, the sexes. One such issue was the Voting Rights Act of 1965, which guaranteed voting privileges to blacks. Rosa Parks is considered the mother of the civil rights movement.

Parks suffered for many years as a result

of her action, but eventually she received hundreds of honors for her stand, including the Congressional Gold Medal, awarded in 1999 to Parks by the U.S. Congress. In his citation President Bill Clinton stated, "Forty-three years ago in Alabama . . . Rosa Parks boarded a public bus, took a seat, and began a remarkable journey." It was a journey that resulted in more changes than Parks could have imagined.

1

A Remarkable Journey

The moment is frozen in Rosa Parks's mind. World War I had just ended and soldiers were coming home from the battle-fields in France. The year was 1919 and she was around six years old. She was frail and sickly and lived in a tiny rural community called Pine Level, Alabama. The little hamlet lay in Alabama's Black Belt, located about thirty miles south of Montgomery and named for its rich black soil. At the time, Parks was still Rosa McCauley. She lived on an eighteen-acre farm with her mother, Leona McCauley, her baby brother, Sylvester, and her grandparents.

It was an ordinary day until the visitors came. Young Rosa knew Moses Hudson. He and his wife owned the big plantation next door to her family's farm. Hudson was a white man. This meant Rosa's family would have to act differently than usual around him. They would have to show polite respect at all times. Their lives could depend upon it.

Hudson had a young man with him, a white soldier in uniform. Hudson presented the young man as his son-in-law and said he was from the North. When Rosa was introduced to the soldier, he patted her on the head and remarked that she was a cute little girl. This kind gesture was so unusual in that place and time that Parks never forgot it.

"One of my earliest memories of childhood is hearing my family talk about the remarkable time that a white man treated me like a regular little girl, not a little black girl," Parks wrote nearly seventy years later. Her grandfather would laugh and laugh whenever he told the story and say he "saw old Mose Hudson's face turn red as a coal of fire."

Rosa McCauley Parks never forgot being treated like a "regular" little girl. Her daily life was very different. She did not have frequent contact with whites in the village. Segregation of the races was the law of the land in the South at that time.

Segregation meant that black and white

children attended separate schools and worshiped in separate churches. Children of different races usually didn't play together. If they did, there were rules for that, too.

Rosa was born on February 4, 1913, in Tuskegee, Alabama. Her mother believed her children would get a good education in Tuskegee, a fairly large town with a well-known college for blacks. But her husband, James, was more interested in what he believed he could earn there as a carpenter, bricklayer, and stonemason.

The young family lived near the Tuskegee Institute, which had been founded for blacks in the early 1880s by a former Virginia slave named Booker T. Washington. The best-known professor at the school was George Washington Carver. A former slave as well, Carver became famous for developing many uses for sweet potatoes and peanuts, crops which replenished the soil of the area. (Children today know Carver as the creator of peanut butter.)

At the time of Rosa McCauley's birth, the school was a place of special opportunity for African-Americans. There were vast rolling fields, well-maintained buildings, and a library that blacks could use. The Tuskegee

Institute was one of the few places in the South where African-Americans could learn skills and get an education.

Rosa's mother wanted to stay in Tuskegee, and she taught in the area for as long as she could. But her husband was drawn by stories of better salaries in the North and went to explore. When he returned, he moved his family from Tuskegee to Abbeville, nearly a hundred miles away, to live with his folks.

But soon he took off for the North again. Rosa was still a toddler and there was another baby on the way. Soon, Rosa's mother packed the family's things and moved from Abbeville back to her parents' home in Pine Level. James McCauley rejoined them a couple of times, then went north when Rosa was five. After that, Rosa didn't see her father again until she was a married adult. Her parents never reunited.

Life in Pine Level was poor in material goods but rich in love and connections to family members of many generations. These things would help Rosa through trying periods later in her life.

Pine Level offered many natural wonders. Rosa loved to go fishing with her grandmother at a nearby creek, where silver fish darted, swam, and sometimes — when the creeks ran high — leaped all the way out of the muddy brown water.

Rosa had to watch out for snakes, especially cottonmouth water moccasins. They were highly poisonous snakes that loved the swamps and creek banks of the south. (The dark snakes got their names from the white interiors of their mouths. A moccasin could hold its tail erect and wiggle it like a caterpillar to attract prey. Even today water moccasins are a threat to fishermen. And even today the bites can be deadly.)

Rosa learned to sew and became quite good at it. She especially liked to sew scraps of cloth into the squares that would become a quilt top and, eventually, a quilt. Rosa McCauley had lots of patience. She knew how to make something out of nothing and how to wait for what she wanted. There was no scrap too small to be of some use, and even tiny scraps pieced together could always be turned into something significant.

Quilting bees were common winter social events for southern farmwomen near Pine Level. They would put their scraps into their wagons and ride off to meet at someone's home during the last stages of quilt making.

Then the assembled quilters would add the backing, place cotton inside, and sew swirls of fine stitches to hold the cotton in place.

Rosa McCauley might have wanted to attend all the local quilting bees. But her swollen, infected tonsils limited what she could do. There was always a danger they would they serve as a breeding ground for other, life-threatening diseases. Antibiotics did not exist and surgery was highly risky even in a city, much less in the countryside. So Rosa often stayed home from school, especially in the winter. She was often too frail to walk the long distances to the ramshackle, one-room structures that served as schools for African-Americans. To attend one school she had to walk eight miles each way.

Elderly Pine Level residents still tell stories of how much Rosa resented walking past the new school buildings for whites on her long hike to the closest school for blacks. The black schools were not an inspiring sight. Often their little shuttered windows held no glass. Usually there were no desks.

Instead, parents cut small logs to serve as stools and sometimes nailed on small boards to serve as seat backs. Heat came from a wood stove set in the middle of the room.

Lunch was whatever one brought: cornbread and onions, or biscuits with fatback (fatty bacon) for the fortunate. Students hoisted up buckets of cold water from a well, plunged a dipper into the bucket for a drink, then sipped from the dipper, which all the children and the teacher shared.

Books were in short supply and usually came as castoffs from schools for whites. By the time they arrived, books often lacked crucial pages and were torn and tattered.

At the farm, however, Rosa was surrounded by the love of her grandparents. She learned to rely on herself, her resolve, and Psalm 27:

The Lord is my light and my salvation; whom shall I fear? The Lord is the strength of my life; of whom shall I be afraid? . . . When my father and my mother forsake me, then the Lord will take me up . . . Wait on the Lord, be of good courage, and He shall strengthen thine heart: wait, I say, on the Lord.

The Bible was often the only book in local households. The lessons of the Bible were often mixed with those of daily life.

Parks never forgot what she learned in

Pine Level. At a large gathering many years later, Parks recited a hymn her mother sang to her as a child:

> *"Oh, freedom,*
> *Oh, freedom over me,*
> *Before I'd be a slave*
> *I'd be buried in my grave*
> *And go home to my Lord."*

Rosa's favorite psalm asked, "Whom shall I fear?" and she knew the answer — white men, white men on horseback, riding in the middle of the night — the Ku Klux Klan.

Founded in Pulaski, Tennessee, in 1866, by Nathan Bedford Forrest, a renowned former Confederate general, the KKK worked first to return control of the South to the hands of the former slaveholders. Then Klansmen employed a wide range of violence to spread fear and discourage voters from supporting candidates who weren't sponsored by the Klan.

Most KKK victims were blacks, particularly blacks who tried to vote or to become politically active. Tactics ranged from warnings, such as explosions or cross-burnings, to murder. The Klan particularly targeted northern schoolteachers who came south to teach blacks, who had been prevented by law from learning to read and write during slavery.

During Rosa's childhood, the KKK began to really grow in Alabama. The group held huge membership drives in cities such as Birmingham and Montgomery, the latter only thirty miles up the gravel highway from Pine Level.

During these years, Parks has written that she often lay awake in terror, listening to the sound of horses' hooves going past on the road outside, knowing that her grandfather was sitting up, awake, with his shotgun on his lap, in case the KKK decided to stop at their house. After all, they owned land and were "uppity" — they didn't "stay in their place."

And, even as a small child, Rosa McCauley knew she had crossed the color line as well. When she was about 10, she met a little white boy named Franklin on her road. He threatened to hit Rosa so she picked up a brick and dared him to hit her. That frightened the little bully off.

When Rosa told her grandmother about it, she expected her grandmother to be pleased. Instead, Rosa's grandmother became upset with *her*. Not only did she say Rosa shouldn't have threatened the white child, she said she should not have fought back even if she were hit. Then she told Rosa that if she weren't careful, she'd likely be lynched (hanged by the Klan) before she was twenty.

Little Rosa would lie awake in the dark, listening to her beating heart as the Klan rode by, thinking about all the things she'd already done to anger them. Rosa McCauley would carry this memory with her when she left Pine Level, and it would flash before her again at another terrifying point in her life.

2
Simple Actions

Somehow Rosa's mother, Leona McCauley, managed to obtain a scholarship for Rosa to attend Miss White's School for Girls. It was in the city of Montgomery, thirty miles from tiny Pine Level, and Rosa would have to live in the city, far away from her family. But it was the best chance for young Rosa to get a solid education. Miss White's School had been founded after the Civil War, when many northern women traveled south to teach the newly freed slaves.

The teachers took risks to do this work. Local men and women in their age groups shunned them. They could expect none of the famous southern hospitality. Sometimes teachers were beaten, occasionally they were killed. Miss White's School was burned down twice in its early years. Poorer whites, who had little education themselves, doubly resented the teachers' coming south to teach blacks.

Miss White had moved to Montgomery from Massachusetts. Sears probably supported her school. (Julius Rosenwald, the president of Sears, Roebuck and Co., a big mail-order catalogue company, provided money to build many one-room schoolhouses for black children in the South.) There were approximately three hundred students at Miss White's, which occupied a three-story building on Union Street.

At Miss White's, Rosa McCauley mastered far more than the standard reading, writing, and arithmetic. She learned to speak correctly, in a refined voice. She developed her penmanship and began to write in a lovely style. She also learned manners appropriate for city life.

As Rosa was growing and learning, though, here she encountered the most maddening aspects of segregation. Pine Level had been too small to provide any drinking fountains, much less separate ones for blacks and whites. Alabama weather was so hot in the summer that your clothes would stick to your body. People traveled long distances in open wagons, and clouds of dust were kicked up by the horses and mules that pulled them. Public drinking fountains were a necessity, yet each one had a sign over it: "Whites Only" or "Colored."

Segregation affected practically everything African-Americans did. It affected where they went and how they acted. There were even rules about which doors blacks and whites might use to enter some buildings.

Pine Level had been too poor to provide separate building entrances for different races. But in Montgomery, the races were sometimes even confined to different floors.

Trolleys and streetcars ran on tracks throughout downtown Montgomery. Like the city buses that would come later, trolleys and streetcars were segregated. African-Americans had to ride as far back in the cars as possible. Rosa McCauley and her aunt rarely took public transportation; mostly, they walked.

Services were divided as well. Restaurants were for whites or blacks, not both. Medical care was very hard to come by if you were black. There *were* African-American undertakers and ministers plus a small group of businesspeople who provided services, such as shoe repair shops, diners, barber shops, and hair salons. Yet any establishment that might produce a high profit, like a grocery store or a clothing store, usually remained in the hands of whites. If blacks tried to compete, they were threatened. If that didn't work, their stores often mysteriously burned down.

Rosa McCauley loved books. There were books in Montgomery, but often she could not *get* to them. Either they were kept in public libraries, which were not open to blacks, or they were sold in bookstores for sums that a poor schoolgirl had no chance of saving. The world beckoned to black children in Montgomery but the entrances were all locked.

Rosa's scholarship carried some responsibilities: She cleaned two classrooms after school each day. Rosa boarded with her mother's older sister, Fannie Williamson, who was in poor physical health. She, also, needed Rosa's help at her job.

Unlike Rosa's mother, Fannie had gotten married and gone to work instead of pursuing her education as her parents wanted. Now she had a job cleaning a country club in Montgomery.

So, after going to school all day and dusting and sweeping two classrooms, Rosa then joined her aunt and helped clean the country club. Then there was homework. There was seldom any time for play. Every once in a while, for a treat, Rosa played ball a little or picked fat and juicy blackberries when they came in season.

There was no public high school for blacks in the capital city, so Rosa attended ninth grade at Booker T. Washington Junior High. Alabama State Teachers' College for Negroes did offer a laboratory school, however, where new teaching methods were used and evaluated. Rosa attended the tenth grade there and began the eleventh.

Then Rosa's grandmother became very ill, and Rosa dropped out of high school to care for her. Her grandmother died about a month later, so Rosa McCauley returned to Montgomery, where she worked in a shirt factory. Then her mother got sick and Rosa returned to Pine Level once again.

The window on a better life seemed to have closed. Several years passed as Rosa nursed her mother and kept the farm going. Then one day a young white man knocked on the farm door. His name was Raymond Parks.

3

Struggling Together

Rosa McCauley had already met Raymond Parks briefly when someone she knew introduced them in Montgomery. Raymond worked as a barber in a downtown Montgomery shop. In one of her books, Rosa wrote that at first she had no interest in Parks because she "thought he was too white." While Raymond looked white, he also had African-American ancestors. By the racial rules of the day, that made him black.

Raymond suffered greatly because of his skin color. He was too light to be a black man, and sometimes this caused him problems from both blacks and whites.

The whole issue of color was confusing and difficult to explain in a sensible way. "White" referred to people whose skin color appeared pink to light yellow or brown *if* the person was not known to have any African-American ancestry. If the person was known or suspected to have any African-American relatives, he or she was considered "black."

Black people were seldom ebony-colored enough to look black because there had been so much mixing of races. In appearance, "blacks" ranged from white to tan to brown to ebony. Yet no matter how much white ancestry a person had, if he or she was suspected to have *any* African-American ancestry, the person was considered black.

Raymond Parks was a man much like Rosa's relatives. He had always had trouble with the color issue. Rosa even had a grandfather who looked as white as Raymond Parks — and he'd had just as much trouble because of his color.

Raymond had a difficult time finding Rosa's house. When he stopped to ask blacks where she lived, they wouldn't tell him because they thought he was white. In those days, it was not usually a good sign when a white went looking for a black.

Rosa McCauley and Raymond Parks had an important thing in common. Both had a deep desire to make life better for African-Americans.

One thing that really impressed Rosa about Raymond was his involvement in the Scottsboro case.

This case was a major civil rights issue for nearly twenty years. A fight had broken out between a large group of black and white men aboard a train in 1931. The sheriff at the next stop, Scottsboro, Alabama, took nine black youths off the train and filed serious charges against them; the sheriff said two women aboard the train stated that they had been sexually attacked. Evidence was weak but all nine black youths were convicted by an all-white jury. Many people believed they were innocent, and the trial became a world-wide issue. People in Alabama particularly followed the case because it took place there.

Raymond Parks kept Rosa McCauley informed about this famous trial as it progressed. He helped raise money for the defense of the men and for the appeals that followed their convictions. Rosa Parks said later that Raymond was the first man with whom she had ever discussed the racial situation or the problems it caused.

Rosa McCauley and Raymond Parks were married at her mother's home in Pine Level in 1932. Then they moved to Montgomery. But the Great Depression was in full swing and survival for blacks, never easy, became even harder.

Rosa Parks sewed for people. She worked for the Metro Life Insurance Company, and was a clerk for a time. She also returned to and completed high school in 1934, when she was twenty-one. Her new husband encouraged her.

Raymond Parks remained involved in the defense effort in the Scottsboro case, which continued for many years. He brought the young men food when they were in jail in Montgomery.

There was great danger in being involved in the Scottsboro defense. Meeting places were kept secret, guards were posted to look out for whites, and some people carried guns. After Raymond and Rosa were married, he sometimes would sneak home through back ways after meetings. She would wait up for him, terrified that the Klan would find out and waylay him.

Later she described a time the Scottsboro committee met at their tiny house. She said she went outside, sat down on the back steps, and put her head down for the whole meeting.

"I was very, very depressed about the fact that black men could not even hold a meeting without fear of bodily injury or death," she said.

After a third trial in 1936–1937, charges against four young men were dropped but five served long prison terms, one lasting until 1950.

When Rosa graduated from high school, she was a well-trained secretary. However, there were no jobs available for black secretaries in Montgomery. Whites wouldn't hire blacks as secretaries and blacks, relegated to the lowest-paying jobs, seldom needed them. Her mother wanted her to become a teacher, but Rosa had seen the hardships and the poor pay teachers received.

Because Rosa was an excellent seamstress, she eventually obtained a job sewing. She became the assistant men's tailor for the Montgomery Fair Department Store, the best department store in the city.

At that time, African-Americans generally could not try on clothing in white department stores, but instead had to guess whether a garment might fit. Even if clothing didn't fit, blacks couldn't return it. Yet African-Americans could still alter clothing to fit white customers (just as they could cook food for whites but could not eat with them).

Eventually, the Parks couple moved into an apartment building called Cleveland Gardens. Leona McCauley came to live with them. Raymond Parks began barbering in a privately owned shop at nearby Maxwell Air Force Base.

Long interested in advancing the rights of African-Americans, Rosa Parks began joining political organizations. Just as her ancestors had often refused to bow to the demands of segregation, Rosa resolved to do what she could to end the practice. In 1943 she became one of the first women to join the Montgomery chapter of the National Association for the Advancement of Colored People (NAACP). The NAACP was one of the most active national organizations working to extend full rights of citizenship to blacks. In the South merely joining the group could be dangerous. Raymond Parks had long been a member of the Montgomery chapter but, because of the danger, hadn't especially encouraged his wife to join.

Rosa thought there were no women in the organization until she saw Mrs. Johnnie Carr's name mentioned in a publication. Carr, one of Rosa's classmates at Miss White's School, served as the NAACP secretary. So Rosa Parks decided to attend a meeting.

She attended the December 1943 meeting to elect officers. Carr was not present and, when the all-male group looked around for a woman to take notes, Rosa Parks was not only selected, she was elected secretary. There was no pay. But from then on, Rosa Parks was at the center of what went on to advance the rights of African-Americans in Montgomery. She not only typed letters, she organized meetings and contacted key speakers. She wrote and distributed leaflets to let the black community know what was happening. Although her race kept her from holding jobs for which she was qualified, she was becoming a woman of considerable power.

4

A Ringing Rebuke

NAACP president, E. D. Nixon, noticed that Rosa Parks never missed a meeting. After working all day at the tailor shop, Parks would often eat dinner and then — taking a sandwich for Nixon — go over to his office where there was a typewriter, and type a few letters.

Nixon had a job that was highly prized among African-Americans of the time. He was a Pullman porter on one of the railroad lines. He looked after the needs of train passengers who traveled overnight and booked a bed — called a berth — in a sleeping car, a Pullman named for George M. Pullman, its inventor. The pay was good and, more important, the job got Nixon out of Montgomery. That meant whites there could not deny

Nixon a job to punish his efforts to advance the rights of blacks (this was the most effective weapon whites had to keep blacks quiet about segregation). With this measure of freedom, Nixon became a fine leader and one of the most influential citizens in Alabama.

Rosa Parks also volunteered for the Montgomery Voters League, which encouraged blacks to register and vote. The Voters League often met in the Parks' house and, between meetings, Rosa did some typing for the group.

Voting for leaders in elections is one of Americans' most important rights. But, for a very long time, most people in the United States were kept from voting and African-Americans were kept from voting the longest. Many blacks served in World War I, believing voting rights would follow; they did not. Many blacks served in World War II, including Rosa's brother Sylvester, who came back from the war, moved to Detroit, and never returned to Pine Level. Still, few blacks were allowed to vote. But this time, they began to organize and to keep records of each attempt.

Rosa Parks repeatedly tried to register to vote, but all the people in charge were whites who required would-be voters to read and interpret a difficult passage from the U.S. Constitution. They used this passage to automatically approve whites, but they almost always turned blacks down.

Voting had long been a privilege for only some voters. In the beginning of our nation's history, only white males who owned property could vote. Eventually the property requirement was dropped, but still only white males could vote. In 1870, after the Civil War, the voting privilege was extended to black men. However, well-to-do white men devised a new method to bar black men and poorer white men from voting: the poll tax, a payment of one to three dollars that men had to pay before they could vote. This kept many blacks from voting because wages were low and some workers only made fifty cents per day. There was another catch to the poll tax law — a would-be voter had to pay the tax all the way back to the year he turned 21. He also had to carefully keep the receipts and take them each time or he would be denied the right to vote even if he had already paid the tax.

In 1920, after many years of trying, women gained the right to vote. However, they, too, had to pay the poll tax. Many women worked in the home and had no money of their own. Sometimes husbands could not or *would* not pay the poll taxes for their wives to vote. Sometimes a husband expected his wife to vote for the same candidate as he did.

By the time Rosa Parks began trying to vote, new voters had to pass a test on government before voting. People giving the tests would often change the answers and rig the tests so only those who supported the politicians in charge could vote.

The second time Parks tried to vote, she was turned down again. But something else happened, too: She was forced off a city bus. It was an all-too-common event at the time, but its effects would spin out, like the ripples that keep going when you throw a rock in a pond.

Montgomery buses were not only segregated, drivers also were armed. They could and did use their weapons on occasion to enforce all the rules governing segregation on buses.

One rule was that blacks could enter at the front *only* to pay their fares. Then they had to get off the bus, go around to the back door, and get back on. After they headed to the back door, some drivers would just drive off and leave them. Other white bus drivers were kinder and allowed blacks to pay their fares, then go right through the white section to the back. But one of the worst effects of segregation was the way it allowed racist people to do bad things to blacks without being punished.

The bus company also reserved the first ten rows on each bus for whites, whether any were on the bus or not. As long as no more than ten rows of whites rode the bus, African-Americans could sit in the remaining seats. On a full bus, however, if a white entered after a black had sat down, the black had to get up and move farther back. If there were no remaining seats, the black had to just stand up. Some blacks just got off and walked rather than move back.

Many more blacks than whites rode the buses in Montgomery. And most riders were women, because they earned less than men and were less likely to own cars. Most whites had automobiles, but blacks often rode the bus at least twice daily. And nearly all of Montgomery's black residents had stories to tell about bad treatment.

On the same day that Rosa Parks was turned down again for voting, she had the misfortune of getting on a bus with the kind of driver African-Americans feared most.

It was a winter day and Parks entered the bus, paid her fare, and walked through an empty white section to the back, where many African-Americans were crowded. When she looked back, however, the driver was standing and staring at her.

The driver called back and ordered her to get off and get on at the back. Rosa Parks told the driver she was already on the bus and pointed out that it was crowded and would be difficult to get through the crowd and back to the door. Then she stayed where she was.

The driver didn't. He came back and grabbed her coat sleeve. As she moved forward, she dropped her purse and sat down momentarily in a white seat to pick it up. He began yelling at her, she wrote later, and he looked ready to hit her.

"I know one thing," Parks said. "You better not hit me."

He didn't. She had already gotten a transfer so she got off that bus and took another. As she left the bus, Rosa could hear complaints among the blacks, comments like, "She ought to go around." After this incident, Rosa always looked to see who a driver was before boarding a bus, and she avoided that particular driver for twelve years.

In the meantime, she studied harder for her voting test. She decided to write down all her answers the next time she took the test. Then, if she were turned down, she would have a record to use to question the result.

Parks had already considered filing a lawsuit if the voting officials did not pass her, but there were very few black attorneys in Alabama at the time. There *was* a black attorney in New York who came from Alabama. His name was Arthur A. Madison and he sometimes came down to Alabama and worked with the NAACP to help people register to vote. At one point, he was arrested for his voter registration efforts.

But on her third try, the registrar decided to pass Rosa Parks. She had to pay a poll tax of $1.50 for each year back to the time she was twenty-one. By that time she was thirty-two and her tax was approximately $18.00, more than many people made in a week. But Rosa was prepared and paid her tax.

Each time Parks joined an organization, she did what she always did: She went to work. Whether it was the local or state NAACP Branch or the Voters League, she could be depended upon to get the work done. Other people were always president, others made speeches, but Parks was the one who took the notes during meetings, answered mail, and typed letters of protest.

E. D. Nixon, the NAACP president, was probably the single most active and well-connected African-American in Montgomery. For years, Nixon was president of either the Montgomery or state branch of the NAACP or both, and Parks served alongside as secretary. Eventually she worked with Nixon in other activities. He maintained an office as state NAACP president and as a regional officer for the Brotherhood of Sleeping Car Porters, a powerful union of the African-Americans who managed the sleeping cars on the railroads.

Nixon spent many years involved in union work with national African-American leaders. He worked with A. Philip Randolph, who started the union because whites barred blacks from railroad unions, and Bayard Rustin, who worked for a group called the Fellowship of Reconciliation. Eventually, Nixon hired Parks to assist him in these other projects. In each case Parks came to know state and national leaders of the organizations. Her activities by now extended far beyond secretarial assistance.

When black citizens filed reports of beatings or other violence, Parks was frequently the person who interviewed them. When she could find witnesses, she talked to them. Afterward, she compiled reports of her findings, and the organizations would try to take some form of action. From 1943 onward, Rosa Parks was involved in some way with practically every issue that came to the attention of the civil rights groups.

Nixon spent much of his life challenging the idea that blacks should "stay in their place," meaning they should leave all the decisions and desirable jobs to whites. Yet, he thought that *women* should "stay in their place," leaving the well-paying jobs and leadership positions to men. This attitude did not please Parks, who continually provided the backup work that Nixon needed.

"He used to say, 'Women don't need to be nowhere but in the kitchen,'" Parks has written. "I would ask him, 'Well, what about me?' He would respond, 'But I need a secretary and you are a good one.'"

Despite Nixon's attitudes toward women, Parks ended up with ever-expanding responsibilities. Since Nixon was a railroad porter, he was out of town much of the time and impossible to reach on trains. Rosa Parks was the person everyone dealt with in Nixon's absence.

She made decisions and kept the operations going. Nixon later told an interviewer that once, when something happened that Parks thought needed an instant response, she sent a letter out with his name on it. He was across the country and didn't find out about it until later.

Parks worked at lunch, after work, and on weekends. She organized committees and meetings and distributed the notices to churches and meeting places. She came to know virtually everybody involved in efforts to advance the rights of blacks in Montgomery. They knew who Parks was, too.

Her network of contacts also included some whites who were interested in helping African-Americans. For instance, Nixon introduced Parks to Virginia and Clifford Durr, a local couple who both came from wealthy families in Montgomery. Clifford Durr was one of the few white attorneys in the city who took black clients.

Virginia Durr had organized a prayer

group of white and black women; they met in Durr's home and Parks began to attend. The Durrs had very little money because whites would not do business with them, but Virginia Durr's sister was married to Hugo Black, a Justice of the U.S. Supreme Court, the highest court in the land. In May of 1954, the U.S. Supreme Court decided that schools throughout the country should be integrated. This decision came about in the *Brown v. Board of Education of Topeka, Kansas* case. This meant that black children all over the country, including places like Pine Level, could attend the same schools as their white neighbors. African-Americans were overjoyed. They believed that whites would accept the decision. There was great celebration in the black communities across the land.

Many whites were outraged. They wanted to keep the races apart. If black and white children attended school together, they would be more likely to "mix," to become friends, perhaps neighbors, and maybe even marry each other. In Alabama, the Ku Klux Klan began to rally and ride again, this time in automobiles instead of on horseback.

In the fall of 1954, a few African-American children were selected to enter the formerly all-white school across the street from the Durrs'.

Rosa Parks did not have any children but she set about helping the African-American children integrate the school. She did not have a car, so she rode the bus back and forth to help them.

She tutored the children and helped them obtain proper clothes and textbooks. Some of the children came from well-to-do homes and had good training. However, some of the children had had very poor schooling.

Some white teachers, upset at having to teach African-Americans, mimeographed the papers of black students who did poorly and passed them around as examples of the kind of students they had to teach.

As a result of her constant volunteering to do one little job after the other, Rosa Parks had become even more well known in the African-American community. Everywhere she went, African-Americans recognized her.

She also came in contact with many of the national leaders in the African-American community. When they came through Montgomery, they usually had dealings with E. D. Nixon. Rosa Parks, as usual, took care of the details.

She was also skilled at developing contacts who might be helpful to her cause. Alabama African-Americans who wanted to attend law school had to go out of state in those days, and when a local young man named Fred Gray returned to set up his law practice, Parks paid attention. The legal system in Alabama often treated blacks unfairly. Blacks could not even attend law school in the state. Thus there were only a handful of black lawyers in the state.

Soon Parks was taking a sandwich over to Gray's office at lunchtime. She began typing a few letters for the young attorney. They would talk while they ate. Gray, too, was determined to help end segregation.

"At lunchtime, Mrs. Parks often walked to my office, located one-and-a-half blocks from the Montgomery Fair department store where she worked as a seamstress," Gray wrote later in his book, *Bus Ride to Justice*. "We became very good friends."

The two of them discussed the situation of Claudette Colvin, a fifteen-year-old student who had been arrested in the spring of 1955 for refusing to give up her bus seat to a white woman. Parks took a particular interest in Colvin's case, not only because of the bus issue but because Colvin was the great-granddaughter of a Pine Level black man who had refused to work for white men.

In addition to attorney Gray, Parks met with Colvin and NAACP head Nixon, and a college teacher, Jo Ann Robinson, another woman who was determined to do something about the segregated buses. Robinson was a college professor at Alabama State College and she, too, had an awful experience on a Montgomery bus.

Robinson had a car and did not normally take the bus. But in December of 1949, Robinson left her car at home and boarded a bus to go to the airport. She was going to Ohio to visit friends and family for Christmas. There were only two people on the bus, she said, a white woman in the third row from the front and a black man in a seat near the back. Distracted by her thoughts about her trip, Robinson sat down in the fifth row from the front and closed her eyes.

Suddenly, she heard yelling. When she opened her eyes, she saw that the bus driver had turned in his seat and was yelling at her.

He left his seat and stood over Robinson with his hand drawn back.

"'Get up from there!'" he yelled, she said

in her book, *The Montgomery Bus Boycott, and the Women Who Started It.* "He repeated it, for, dazed, I had not moved. 'Get up from there!'"

Robinson jumped up and, without thinking, ran to the front door, instead of the back door, where blacks were supposed to go. The driver opened the door, and she walked back to the college. A friend took her to the airport.

Robinson said the incident spoiled her holiday.

"In all these years I have never forgotten the shame, the hurt, of that experience," she said in her book, published nearly forty years later.

Robinson was a member of an active group called the Women's Political Council. She told the organization her story; she became president the next year and was president for a number of years after.

"It was during the period of 1949–1955 that the Women's Political Council of Montgomery . . . prepared to stage a bus boycott when the time was ripe and the people were ready," Robinson wrote.

In the meantime, the group wrote letters and met with city officials to try to get changes made, but the government would not budge.

Much discussion took place between Robinson and Parks and Nixon and Gray about using the Colvin arrest as a test case. By pleading not guilty and forcing the city to take the case to court, they could ask a judge to set aside the law requiring segregation on the buses. If they didn't win in Alabama, they could go to a higher court where they might get a favorable decision. So they began raising money to take the case to court. When they discovered Colvin had personal problems the other side would likely use to damage the case, they decided to wait until someone else was arrested. Most people were afraid of the police and followed the segregation order. However, more and more people were getting fed up with the situation on the buses.

Parks continued to meet with Gray.

"Mrs. Parks shared my feelings that something had to be done to end segregation on the buses," Gray wrote. "She gave me the feeling that I was the Moses that God had sent to Pharaoh and commanded him to 'Let my people go.' She saw that I was penniless and she wanted to help me get on my feet."

Parks knew hardship only too well. Her husband, Raymond, was in bad health and could not always work. Getting by on Rosa Parks's small salary was very hard indeed.

By this time Parks had yet another responsibility: She was the advisor to the NAACP's Youth Council. She organized a high school group to challenge less dangerous but damaging types of segregation. They particularly challenged the segregated library system. Blacks were not allowed to check out books from the white libraries. Instead, they could only obtain books from a small *colored* library, which had few books. If they wanted a particular book which the colored library did not have, they could request it from one of the white libraries. This was time-consuming and humiliating. Blacks might have to walk or ride a long distance to the library for blacks, sometimes passing by the library for whites. Youth Council members regularly went to white libraries and requested books; over and over, they were turned down. Nonetheless, young people were learning early to challenge the system of segregation.

In the summer of 1955, Parks was offered a special opportunity: a scholarship to attend the Highlander Folk School in Monteagle,

Rosa Parks is fingerprinted in jail.

Rosa Parks walks up the courthouse steps in Montgomery.

Dr. Martin Luther King, Jr. speaks at the Holt Street Baptist Church.

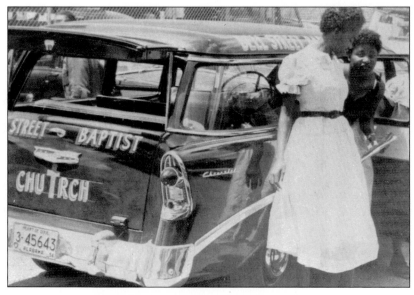

During the Montgomery boycott, church-operated station wagons like these took people around the city.

Montgomery streets were full of empty buses during the boycott.

Rosa Parks sits in the front of a Montgomery bus.

The Reverend Jesse Jackson with Rosa Parks at the dedication of the National Civil Rights Museum in Memphis, 1991.

Rosa Parks wears the Presidential Medal of Freedom awarded to her by President Bill Clinton in 1996.

Tennessee. The school was founded during the 1930s to train workers to organize and demand better wages and working conditions. Later, it trained civil rights leaders.

Miles Horton, who founded the school, constantly looked for new leaders to train. He and Virginia Durr had worked together against the poll tax. When Horton called Durr and asked her to suggest someone from Montgomery for the scholarship, she thought of Rosa Parks right away.

Attending Highlander was a milestone in Parks's life. In *Eyes on the Prize,* a book on the civil rights movement, Parks said her experience at Highlander was the first time in her whole life that she had been in a truly integrated setting.

"It was a place I was very reluctant to leave," she said. "I gained there strength to persevere in my work for freedom, not just for blacks but all oppressed people."

There were workshops on labor unions, workers' rights, voting rights, and race relations. Parks was greatly affected by Highlander, and Miles Horton always took great pride in the fact that Parks had attended his school.

Parks returned to Montgomery and continued to type letters and set up meetings, to advise the youth group, and to help voters register. Almost every day it seemed there was word of new violence against blacks, if not in Alabama, then elsewhere across the South. As blacks organized to go after their rights, many whites organized to block the changes.

The Ku Klux Klan was forming new groups all over the South, and a powerful new organization, the White Citizens Council, formed soon after the U.S. Supreme Court decided to end segregation in schools. Unlike the Klan, the White Citizens Council was made up of wealthier whites. Many southern governors and some southern members of Congress joined.

Violence increased throughout 1955. The Rev. George Lee, one of the first blacks to register to vote, urged his congregation to do the same and was murdered in Mississippi, the state next to Alabama. Lamar Smith organized blacks to vote and soon after was shot to death by a white on a Mississippi courthouse lawn. Dozens of people watched, yet no one would admit to having seen the crime! Often blacks who had not "stayed in their place" would simply disappear. Their bodies might never be found.

The NAACP and the Women's Political Council (WPC) continued to watch for a bus arrest that they could use for a court case. They believed the law was unjust and would be struck down once the case reached higher courts outside Alabama. So they watched for the police to arrest someone who would perform well in court. E. D. Nixon was determined to use a case that would win, one that the whites could not influence in some way. Two other women were arrested after Colvin.

"[W]e'd talked about a bus boycott all the year," Nixon told Howell Raines in *My Soul Is Rested*. "I've handled so many cases that I know when a man would stand up and when he wouldn't."

All three of the people who "stood up" and were arrested were women. However, each case presented a factor that could cause a problem, so none of the three arrests became a test case. There is no evidence the groups ever tried to set up a test case themselves by deliberately seeking arrest.

Then, in November, another landmark court case came down from the Supreme Court. A U.S. government agency, the Interstate Commerce Commission, banned segregation on interstate travel. This meant that blacks and whites would ride in the same sections of the buses and trains that traveled between states. It was a great victory. But this decision did not affect city buses.

There was nothing unusual about the first day of December 1955. At lunchtime, Parks walked over to Fred Gray's office, as she often did. They ate their lunches, talked a while, and Parks returned to the department store at 1:00 p.m. Gray finished some work and left town for a few hours to take care of some business.

The tailor shop always had a stack of unfinished sewing waiting to be done. People were beginning to shop for Christmas and the store was busier than ever.

It was the time of year when mothers could hardly pull their children past Montgomery Fair, the major department store in town, only a few blocks from what had been the first capital of the Confederacy. Small children pressed their faces to the display windows, where new toys gleamed and Christmas decorations dazzled workers hurrying home from work.

Past the glitter and the sparkle inside the store, beyond all the expensive clothing, was a hot little room where Parks worked. She had bursitis in her shoulder (soreness probably caused by bending over too much) and it often hurt.

Always neatly dressed with her hair braided and piled atop her head, Parks quickly left Montgomery Fair, picked up a few items across the street, and headed for the nearest bus stop. She was deep in thought about finding a place to hold an upcoming meeting, she said later. When the bus came, Parks stepped on. She forgot about looking to see who the bus driver was before boarding the bus, as she usually did. She had no idea that her next destination would not be home — it would be jail. As a result, life would forever change for African-Americans in the United States.

5

Uncommon Courage

Rosa Parks had already paid her fare when she realized the bus driver was the same one who'd put her off a bus twelve years before. The bus was crowded with blacks standing in the back, but Parks spotted a vacant seat in the middle of the bus, well past the first ten rows reserved for whites. She took her shopping bag and sat down in the seat.

The next stop was at the Empire Theater, a local landmark; some whites boarded and filled all the reserve seats, leaving one white man standing. The driver then called back to Parks and the other three people sitting in her row. "Let me have those front seats," the driver said, according to Parks. The other three African-Americans stood up; Parks merely moved over to the window. "Ya'll better make it light on yourselves and let me have those seats," said the driver, she recalled. Later, Parks said she didn't see how giving in would make it any better for blacks. So she sat still.

When the driver asked her if she were going to get up, Parks simply said, "No."

"He said, 'Well, I'm going to have you arrested.'" She said, "'You may do that.'"

Parks said she did not think about being a test case. She said other passengers began hurrying to get off the bus. The driver got off, called the police and, before long, two officers arrived.

One policeman asked Parks why she didn't get off the bus.

"Why do you all push us around?" she asked.

"I don't know but the law is the law," he replied. "And you're under arrest."

She repeatedly asked to make a phone call and eventually was allowed to do so. She phoned home. Her mother immediately asked if she'd been beaten.

"No," she replied, but her husband needed to come to bail her out. She thought it would be a while, because they did not have a car or the money for the bail.

While Rosa and her mother were talking, a friend who'd heard of the arrest arrived at the Parks's house to see if he could help. Word traveled fast.

"The news [of Parks's arrest] traveled like wildfire into every black home," wrote Jo Ann Robinson, the professor who had enraged a bus driver by sitting in a seat reserved for whites. "Telephones jangled; people congregated on street corners and in homes and talked."

Robinson left messages for Fred Gray, but he was still out of town. E. D. Nixon was working late at his office as usual when his wife phoned. She was excited; she'd learned of Parks's arrest from Bertha Butler, a neighbor who'd seen Parks taken off the bus. When Nixon called the police station to find out the charges, they refused to tell him. He, too, tried to reach Fred Gray and could not. So he called Clifford Durr.

The Durrs had just arrived home and were drinking coffee when Nixon phoned. Nixon asked Durr to find out the charges. He knew the police would tell a white attorney.

"[I]n a few minutes he called me back and

said, 'The charge is violating the Alabama segregation law,'" Nixon later told Raines in *My Soul Is Rested*. The police had made a big mistake. By charging Parks with violating a segregation law, instead of disorderly conduct or a similar charge, they had given her the opportunity to put the issue of segregation on trial.

Nixon asked Clifford Durr to go down with him to make bail.

"Mr. Nixon, I don't have anything to make bail with," Durr replied. Most of Durr's legal clients were too poor to pay, and the Durrs did not even have enough money to own a house.

Nixon said he could make the $100 bail but he needed an attorney to go with him. So the Durrs accompanied Nixon to the jail.

Virginia Durr was the first person Parks saw when she came through the iron door leading from the jail cells.

"There were tears in her eyes and she seemed shaken, probably wondering what they had done to me," Parks remembered in her book. "As soon as they released me, she put her arms around me and hugged and kissed me as if we were sisters."

Nixon paid the bail and by that time Raymond Parks had arrived with some friends. They went to the Parks's house, where Rosa's mother prepared her some food and they all discussed the next step.

Clifford Durr explained that the NAACP could use Parks's arrest to bring a court case to test the legality of the local law requiring segregated buses. They could take her case beyond Alabama, all the way to the U.S. Supreme Court, if she agreed to do so. Nixon was all for the action, of course. Virginia Durr remembered in her book that Rosa Parks was never reluctant about it. However, Durr said her mother and husband were very concerned for Rosa's safety.

Nonetheless, Parks agreed.

Meanwhile, Jo Ann Robinson was up late; this was the best opportunity they'd had for a bus boycott, she later wrote. Robinson and the organization she headed, the Women's Political Council (WPC), had tried to work out changes in bus service for years but city officials refused, and the group had already decided to organize a boycott when the time was right. A boycott would show city officials and the bus company that blacks, who were the majority of bus riders, simply would not ride the buses at all if insulting treatment continued. It would be too late to notify everyone if they waited to have a meeting, Robinson reasoned. They needed to start the boycott Monday morning, December 5, the day of Parks's trial, so officials would see the support for Parks. And to get the word out in time, they would have to get flyers into schools and workplaces on Friday. Fred Gray phoned her at about 11:30 p.m.

"I informed him that I was already thinking that the WPC should distribute thousands of notices calling for all bus riders to stay off the buses on Monday, the day of Mrs. Parks's trial," Robinson told Gray.

" 'Are you ready?' " he asked.

She assured him she was. They hung up and Robinson made notes for a notice and then called the chairman of the business department at the college where she taught. He had access to mimeograph equipment that they could use to print the notices. He agreed to meet her in the middle of the night at the college.

She also called a couple of students and together they ran off over 50,000 notices, enough to let all the Montgomery blacks know of the boycott.

Robinson and other WPC officers had earlier planned how they would distribute notices when time for a boycott came. She set that plan in motion, and was up all night.

She called about thirty people; each of them arranged for others to be in place to receive packets of leaflets. Robinson and her students dropped them off. Bundles were dropped off at schools and students took them home.

"Leaflets were also dropped off at business places, storefronts, beauty parlors, beer halls, factories, and barber shops," Robinson remembered.

E. D. Nixon began calling black ministers when he returned home from the meeting at the Parks's house. Ministers were powerful leaders in the black community — and churches were the only large meeting places that blacks controlled. The third minister on his list was the new minister at the Dexter Avenue Baptist Church, a small, beautifully built church right in the middle of the capital area downtown.

The Dexter Avenue church was considered to have the highest status of the black churches. It had a new minister, a highly educated young man from Atlanta who had gone to school in Boston. His wife was an opera singer of some note. He was 26 years old and unknown, even in Montgomery. His name was Dr. Martin Luther King, Jr.

6

Distance Traveled

Something earth-shattering had happened in Montgomery, though it would be a while before people figured out what it was. One small sign of the change was that Rosa Parks got up the next morning and took a taxi to work. She was no longer going to ride a bus system that treated her badly. She arrived at work on time.

Parks's boss, the white tailor, was surprised. He knew of her arrest — there had been a small article in the morning newspaper. He told Parks he thought she'd be a nervous wreck.

"Why should going to jail make a nervous wreck out of me?" she replied. Indeed, going to jail not only made Parks more determined, it started a fire in the hearts of many African-Americans.

E. D. Nixon had to leave town on a Pullman trip but he set some wheels in motion before he left. The black ministers already had a routine meeting scheduled for that Friday, and Jo Ann Robinson and her WPC officers made sure the boycott notices were dropped off at the meeting site. Black ministers were influential and boycott organizers wanted to gain the ministers' support as soon as possible.

At lunchtime, Parks did as she usually did: She went over to Fred Gray's office and answered his telephone. There was no time for letters. People were calling about the boycott notices and dropping by to hear the latest developments. Montgomery was buzzing. When her lunch hour was over, Parks went back to work.

Before leaving town, Nixon had called for a leadership meeting that Friday night at Dr. Martin Luther King, Jr.'s church. Leaders from virtually every African-American organization were there, including most of the city's black ministers. They agreed to announce the boycott at their churches on Sunday.

The meeting went on without Nixon. "Had E. D. Nixon been present, he would have been automatically selected to preside," King wrote in *Stride Toward Freedom,* "but he had

had to leave town earlier in the afternoon for his regular run on the railroad."

The group agreed to call a citywide meeting of all area African-Americans on Monday night. The boycott would begin Monday morning, December 5, before Parks's court appearance, to demonstrate that the black community was united in demanding changes in the way buses operated. At the Monday night meeting, they would decide whether to extend the boycott.

Indeed, all of Montgomery watched for the buses that Monday. White Montgomery rode alone. Boycott leaders had privately said a sixty percent drop in ridership would be a great success. But when Martin Luther King, Jr. saw bus after bus after bus pass his house with virtually no black riders, he jumped into his car and drove around town looking at the buses. He said he saw no more than eight black passengers in all. "A miracle had taken place," he later wrote.

African-Americans car-pooled. The thirty-five black taxi companies in town offered ten-cent fares — the same as riding the bus — and thousands and thousands of people, mostly women going to cleaning jobs —

walked. And as they walked, they inspired themselves and each other. For the first time, black Montgomery was coming together as never before.

Parks dressed carefully on Monday morning. She was not going to work. Instead, she was making perhaps the most important appearance of her life: She was going to court. She had broken an unjust city law and expected to be found guilty. Then she could appeal the case to a higher court that might set aside the segregation rules for buses.

Parks always dressed well, as her mother had taught her. She worked in the nicest department store in Montgomery and when she couldn't afford to buy a dress, she knew how to make it.

"I remember very clearly that I wore a straight, long-sleeved black dress with a white collar and cuffs, a small black velvet hat with pearls across the top, and a charcoal-gray coat," she wrote. "I carried a black purse and wore white gloves."

She was impeccably dressed for the occasion. White gloves were a badge among white women of the day — Rosa Parks could play the dressing game as well as the political game. She attended to the details, just as she did with her diction and her penmanship, her letters and her organizing.

Parks later said she could hardly see the street for the crowds when she arrived at the courthouse. The NAACP's Youth Council had turned out en masse; they were proud of Parks, their leader. One of the members chanted, "They've messed with the wrong one now."

Fred Gray was there to represent Parks. The white bus driver, James P. Blake, testified and Parks was convicted and fined $10, plus $4 in court fees. This may not sound like much money but it was over half her week's salary of $23 — all to punish her for doing what any white person could do.

Nixon later told an interviewer that he'd been accompanying blacks to court for decades and seldom was there anybody else around, much less a show of support.

"But that particular morning, the morning of December the fifth, 1955, the black man was reborn again . . . people [were] all up and down the streets . . . I looked around and I'll bet you there was over a thousand people — black men — on the streets out there."

And that was just the beginning.

Parks didn't return to the tailor shop that day. She was not a nervous wreck, either. She went over to Fred Gray's office and took messages. While she answered the phone, Nixon and Gray and King and the other ministers held an early meeting. At it, they decided the name of the organization for the boycott would be the Montgomery Improvement Association and that Dr. Martin Luther King, Jr. would be president and Nixon treasurer. Parks, Robinson, and Gray served on the group's executive board.

Nixon later said he wanted King because he'd heard him speak and that King — a new arrival in town — hadn't yet received the kind of favors whites liked to give black leaders to get them on their side.

When the meeting at the Holt Street Baptist Church took place, there was already a sense that something historic was happening. The church and its basement were filled hours before the meeting. Thousands of people stood outside, including Virginia Durr, unable to get inside.

The group overwhelmingly approved the boycott and the actions to organize the effort.

"There is a creative force that works to pull down mountains of evil and hilltops of injustice," Martin Luther King, Jr. wrote of the Holt Street church meeting. "That Monday night was Montgomery's moment in history."

The bus boycott would last approximately 380 days, from December 5, 1955, to December 20, 1956. Along the way there would certainly be mountains of evil and hilltops of injustice, but the boycott continued until the U.S. Supreme Court decided a case that outlawed segregated buses.

Every day of the 380 days required a fresh commitment from the people who needed to ride the buses. While the black taxi companies offered cheap fares, they could not begin to transport the large numbers of people. Those who had cars and never rode the buses, like Virginia Durr, drove car pools. Many people in other states sent money for the group to purchase additional vehicles for the car pools.

The white power structure in Montgomery fought back in every way they could. The police followed taxis and car pools and gave as many tickets as they could. Insurance companies even canceled auto insurance.

Even worse, many whites began to fire workers who boycotted. The Ku Klux Klan spread violence and fear; sometimes they beat up people or bombed their homes. Martin Luther King, Jr.'s house was bombed. So was the home of E. D. Nixon. Rosa Parks received phone calls from people who threatened to kill her. City officials managed to have many boycott leaders arrested, including King, Parks, and others.

In the meantime, Fred Gray filed another court suit, this time involving four people. It asked that bus segregation be declared unconstitutional.

Claudette Colvin was one of the four people included in the case, and it was the one that finally reached the U.S. Supreme Court and ended the city's system of bus segregation.

When the city of Montgomery lost its last appeal of the case, the MIA met again at the Holt Street Baptist Church to formally end the boycott and to celebrate their great victory. "[I]n the long run, it is better to walk . . . than to ride in humiliation," King told the group.

The black ridership returned to the buses the next day. Parks and other leaders were among the first to board and to sit in sections formerly reserved for whites.

By the time the boycott ended, the civil rights movement had spread to other sections of the country. Martin Luther King, Jr. was speaking to thousands of people in city after city every week. Parks was receiving many invitations to rallies as well. She and E. D. Nixon represented the MIA at a gathering at Madison Square Garden in New York, where they appeared with Eleanor Roosevelt, the former First Lady, and A. Philip Randolph, the founder of the Pullman union that had helped Nixon get his start.

Soon, however, Parks would have to begin all over again. Most of the men at the top of the movement had pastored churches. Whites could not put them out of their jobs. Nixon had his Pullman job with the railroad. Fred Gray had his law practice in the black community. But neither Rosa nor Raymond Parks had any hope of employment with whites in Montgomery again. And sooner or later, one of the callers might try to carry out his threats.

With no job prospects in sight at home, Rosa and Raymond Parks decided to move to Detroit, where her brother, Sylvester, had lived since the end of his service in World War II. Sylvester McCauley offered to help get the family resettled. He also rented an apartment for them. The Parkses had little money, so friends in Montgomery raised over $800 for them. The family, including Rosa and Sylvester's mother, Leona, moved to Detroit in 1957.

Getting jobs in Detroit was not easy, either. Barbers there had to be licensed, so Raymond Parks had to return to barber school. In the meantime, he got a job as instructor and maintenance man at the barber school to earn money to pay for his license. Rosa Parks sewed at the home of a friend for a while, but she was still being invited to attend civil rights events around the country.

She would go whenever it was possible. Normally, Parks's expenses were paid but the movement leadership was in the hands of black men now, often ministers, and job openings for black women were still often on the lowest rungs of every ladder.

When Parks met the president of Hampton Institute, a black Virginia college, he offered her a job as a hostess at Holly Tree Inn, a faculty and staff residence.

Parks would be in charge of the four cleaning women who worked half days. Parks took the job, believing the school would provide housing for her family as well. She later said there was an apartment in the nearby annex but officials did not let her have it.

Though she liked the campus and wanted to bring her husband and mother there, Parks never received an apartment and eventually returned to Detroit. She found a job in a small clothing factory there. Sometimes Parks spoke at smaller conventions but, though she attended major events, it was the male leaders who delivered the addresses.

So Parks did what she always did. She went to work — at the clothing factory, in her local organizations, in her community. When the major events in the Civil Rights Movement took place, Parks would try to be a part of them.

When the historic 1963 March on Washington took place, Parks was there. Martin Luther King, Jr. delivered his famous "I Have a Dream" speech and many male leaders spoke.

"Women were not allowed to play much of a role," Parks later wrote of the 1963 march. "The March planning committee didn't want Coretta Scott King and the other wives of the male leaders to march with their husbands. Instead there was a separate procession for them. There were also no female speakers on the program."

Her experiences in Selma, Alabama, were even worse. In 1965, King called for a series of demonstrations in Selma, where blacks were having a difficult time registering to vote. Parks was invited to join the march on its last lap, going into Montgomery. Many famous people were on hand for the march and newspapers and television crews from around the world were on hand to record the event.

Parks was known worldwide as the woman whose actions started the civil rights movement, but to her astonishment, she discovered she was no longer known among the young people in Alabama. Even worse, they kept pushing Parks out of the march.

"Being on that march was a strange experience," she wrote in *Rosa Parks: My Story.* "They didn't know who I was and couldn't care less about me . . . they just kept putting me out of the march, telling me I wasn't supposed to be in it. I got put out of that march three or four times."

Once again, however, they had "messed with the wrong one."

"But I kept getting back in anyway and I

struggled through that crowd until I walked those eight miles to the capitol," Parks said.

When the marchers reached the capitol in Montgomery, where the Confederate flag still flew, leaders called for Parks to go up front and have her picture taken with Roy Wilkins, head of the national NAACP; Ralph Bunche, the first black American winner of the Nobel Peace prize, and other leaders.

"Mostly, I remember being put out of that march," she said.

The past eight years had been difficult. The contrasts in her life were extreme. She was world-famous and might be invited to attend events and be photographed with world leaders. Yet the jobs open to Parks were limited and younger movement members did not necessarily know or care who she was.

So Parks did what she always did. She made something out of nothing again.

7
Promised Land

During the early 1960s, a young man running for Congress in Detroit caught the attention of Rosa Parks. His name was John Conyers, Jr., and he was running as the Democratic candidate for her district in Detroit. Parks liked the issues Conyers raised in his campaign. She decided to help Conyers much as she had helped E. D. Nixon and Fred Gray in Montgomery. When Conyers was elected, the first person he hired for his district office in Detroit was Rosa Parks. This time she was paid for all her actions. She worked as a Congressional aide to Conyers for nearly 24 years, retiring in 1988.

During the 1970s, her mother, brother, and husband all became ill with cancer. Parks nursed them all until their deaths, sometimes working only part-time so she could care for them.

Back in Montgomery, E. D. Nixon was still

powerful. Fred Gray became a noted civil rights attorney and president of the National Bar Association. Like so many young men and women that Parks had helped through the years, he made her proud.

Somewhere along the way, several decades from the time Parks took her historic stand on a bus in Montgomery, something extraordinary began to happen.

It defied reason, as Martin Luther King, Jr. said of the events of the first day of the bus boycott in Montgomery. Yet bit by bit, after years of having been pushed aside from a decision-making role in the civil rights movement, Rosa Parks began to receive the recognition she deserved.

All the little actions she had taken — the phone calls she took on her lunch hour, the letters that she typed for free for men who went on to earn more money and to hold high offices, the meetings she organized and never chaired — seemed to add up. Miraculously, this quiet, soft-spoken, one-time seamstress began to receive honor after honor. She became recognized as the Mother of the Civil Rights Movement.

In early 1981, both Parks and her old friend Virginia Durr received honorary doctor of humane letters degrees from Mt. Holyoke College, a prestigious Massachusetts college. Other degrees followed, from universities from Florida to California.

Cities named streets and parks after the woman who had never headed a major institution or a sizeable group. A street is named for Rosa Parks in Tuskegee, Alabama, where she was born. And in Montgomery, where she boarded the now-famous Cleveland Avenue bus, Cleveland Avenue was renamed Rosa Parks Boulevard. Hundreds of medals and awards were bestowed on Parks in the following years.

In 1987, not long before retiring from Congressman Conyers's office, Parks founded the Rosa and Raymond Parks Institute for Self-Development to carry out her work with young people. Parks continues to work with this organization today.

Years before E. D. Nixon had told journalist Howell Raines, "If Mrs. Parks had got up and given that white man her seat, you'd never aheard of Reverend [Martin Luther] King [the most famous spokesperson for the Civil Rights Movement]."

In 1996, President Bill Clinton bestowed the Presidential Medal of Freedom Award on

Rosa Parks at a White House ceremony. This is the highest award given to American civilians.

"When Rosa Parks refused to give up her seat to a white man on an Alabama bus forty years ago, she ignited the single most significant social movement in American history," Clinton said. "When she sat down on the bus, she stood up for the American ideals of equality and justice and demanded that the rest of us do the same."

In 1998, Troy State University in Montgomery announced that it would build a Rosa Parks Library and Museum at the site of the old Empire Theater, the place where Parks refused to leave her bus seat. Parks lectures twice yearly at the museum.

And, in 1999, what was unthinkable in most years of Parks's life happened: The U.S. Congress voted her its highest award, the Congressional Medal of Freedom. Some of the same members who had blocked important laws giving rights to African-Americans not only voted for Parks to receive the honor, they were on hand when she received it. Only one member of Congress, Representative Ron Paul, a Texas Republican, voted against the medal, saying it was an "unnecessary tax payer expense."

When President Clinton signed the bill giving Parks the medal into law, he told the group how Parks's stand on the bus had inspired him as a small child. As a nine-year-old, he and his friends "began to sit at the back of the bus," Clinton later said.

"Forty-three years ago . . . Rosa Parks boarded a public bus, took a seat, and began a remarkable journey," Clinton said. "Her action that December day, was in itself, a simple one, but it required uncommon courage. It was a ringing rebuke to those who denied the dignity and restricted the rights of African-Americans and it was an inspiration to all Americans struggling together to shed the prejudices of the past and to build a better future. Rosa Parks's short bus trip and all the distance she has traveled in the years since, have brought the American people ever closer to the Promised Land we know it can truly be."

Rosa Parks, appearing in Montgomery several years before, perhaps summed up her actions and her life as well as anyone.

"I'd like for everybody to remember me as a person who wanted to be free," she said.

As a result, millions of people — perhaps all of us — are a bit freer.

Sources

Black Women Oral History Project Interview With Rosa Parks. Boston: Schlesinger Library, Radcliffe College, 1984.

Carson, Clayborne, Senior Editor. *The Papers of Martin Luther King, Jr.* Berkeley, Los Angeles, London: University of California Press, 1997.

Durr, Virginia. *Outside the Magic Circle.* Tuscaloosa: University of Alabama Press, 1985.

Giddings, Paula. *When and Where I Enter.* New York: William Morrow and Company, Inc., 1984.

Graetz, Robert S. *Montgomery: A White Preacher's Memoir.* Minneapolis: Fortress Press, 1991.

Gray, Fred. *Bus Ride to Justice.* Montgomery: Black Belt Press, 1995.

King, Jr., Martin Luther. *Stride Toward Freedom.* New York: Harper & Brothers, 1958.

Morris, Aldon D. *The Origins of the Civil Rights Movement.* New York: The Free Press, 1984.

Myrdal, Gunnar. *An American Dilemma.* New York: Harper & Brothers, 1944.

Parks, Rosa. *Dear Mrs. Parks: A Dialogue With Today's Youth.* New York: Lee & Low, 1996.

Parks, Rosa. *Rosa Parks: My Story.* New York: Dial Books, 1992.

Raines, Howell. *My Soul Is Rested.* New York: G. P. Putnam's Sons, 1977.

Robinson, Jo Ann. *The Montgomery Bus Boycott and the Women Who Started It.* Knoxville: University of Tennessee Press, 1987.

Salmond, John A. *The Conscience of a Lawyer.* Tuscaloosa and London: University of Alabama Press, 1990.

Willams, Juan. *Eyes on the Prize.* New York: Penguin Books, 1987.